Beneath the Facade of

In the stillness, a pulse can be felt,
Under the calm, emotions melt.
Hidden desires dance in the dark,
Yearning for freedom, ready to spark.

To the gentle hum of life we sway,
Beneath the surface, the wild dreams play.
Laughter weaves through whispered fears,
A melody sweet, drying up tears.

Shadows of hope stretch long in the night,
While hearts drum rhythms of pure delight.
In the fragile silence, we find our beat,
A celebration rises, vibrant and sweet.

Through the layers, we reach for the sun,
Beneath the facade, our spirits run.
Together we'll break the gentle disguise,
In this festive moment, our courage will rise.

Vibrations in the Void

In the space where quiet meets the sound,
A pulse of color breaks through the ground.
Whispers of joy ripple in the air,
Creating a rhythm, light as a prayer.

Circles of laughter twirl 'round the night,
Echoes of stories, spirits take flight.
Each note a spark, igniting the dark,
With every heartbeat, we find our mark.

Colors merge in a vibrant play,
Shadows leap, and the stillness sways.
In the void, where silence once reigned,
Vibrations of festivity are unchained.

United we stand, as one in the groove,
The void is alive, our souls start to move.
In this symphony, together we sing,
A chorus of life, joy and everything.

Original title:
Beyond Stillness

Copyright © 2024 Swan Charm
All rights reserved.

Author: Lan Donne
ISBN HARDBACK: 978-9908-1-2236-6
ISBN PAPERBACK: 978-9908-1-2237-3
ISBN EBOOK: 978-9908-1-2238-0

Resurgence of the Unheard

Voices rise like a morning song,
Gathered dreams all yearn to belong.
Banners wave in the jubilant air,
Echoes of hope swirl everywhere.

Laughter spills from the deepest well,
Secrets of joy that we long to tell.
Colors dance as spirits ignite,
Together we shine in the warm twilight.

A tapestry woven with threads of cheer,
Each whisper of love, each heartfelt cheer.
Hands joined together, we take a stand,
For the unheard now rise, united and grand.

In the glow of the festival's light,
The unheard hearts beat strong tonight.
With every beat, new rhythms soar,
Resurgence of voices forevermore.

Fragments of Restlessness

A flicker of laughter in a crowded room,
Fragmented moments begin to bloom.
Whirling emotions weave through the air,
Restlessness dances, shedding its care.

Sparks of connection ignite in our eyes,
In each fleeting glance, our spirits rise.
Shimmering stories beg to be shared,
Amidst the turmoil, we find that we dared.

Rays of delight pierce through the haze,
In the fragments of chaos, we set the blaze.
Colors collide in a festive spree,
A vibrant tapestry, wild and free.

We embrace the unrest, let it take flight,
For in our togetherness, we shine bright.
Fragments unpieced, yet beautifully whole,
Restlessness binds us, heart, spirit, and soul.

Shifting Shadows

In twilight's glow, we twirl and sway,
With laughter bright, we greet the day.
The stars begin their dance in style,
As we embrace the night's sweet smile.

Around the fire, stories unfold,
Of dreams and wishes, brave and bold.
With every cheer, the shadows play,
In festive hearts, they find their way.

The Heart's Quiet Revolution

Beneath the noise, a gentle sound,
Where kindness grows and love is found.
The world alights with colors bright,
As hearts unite, a joyous sight.

In every hug, a spark ignites,
A revolution through the nights.
With every song, we raise our voice,
In festive hearts, we all rejoice.

Voices Beneath the Surface

Whispers linger in the air,
As laughter floats without a care.
The waves of joy, they crash and roar,
In vibrant dances, we explore.

Beneath the stars, secrets entwine,
With every toast, our spirits shine.
In festive dreams, our hopes resound,
With voices deep, our hearts are found.

Unseen Currents

The night is filled with unseen glow,
As friendly faces come and go.
In hidden nooks, affection brews,
With every smile, affection renews.

Around us flow the bonds we weave,
In every moment, we believe.
With whispered joys, the night takes flight,
In festive spirits, all feels right.

The Color of Soundless Dreams

In twilight's embrace we dance,
Under stars that softly gleam.
With laughter that weaves a trance,
Wrapped in joy, a vibrant dream.

Whispers float on gentle breeze,
Carrying notes of sweet delight.
With every step, we aim to seize,
The magic of this festive night.

Sparkling lights and faces bright,
Beneath the moon's warm, radiant glow.
Our hearts ignite, hearts feel so light,
In the rhythm of love, we flow.

So let the evening softly play,
With music painted in the air.
Together we shall drift away,
In moments meant for hearts to share.

Echoes of Untold Reveries

Underneath the shimmering glow,
Dreams awaken, spirits rise.
With every laugh, our joy will flow,
Crafting tales beneath the skies.

Candles flicker, shadows sway,
As we gather, close and near.
In this dance, we find our way,
Chasing echoes, dropping fear.

Cupcakes frosted, laughter shared,
Gifts wrapped in ribbons, hope anew.
Within each smile, love declared,
In every heart, a dream come true.

Let us weave a night of cheer,
With stories spun from laughter's thread.
In this moment, we hold dear,
A world where joy is brightly spread.

The Distance in Between Breathes

Across the room, the laughter flies,
Carried on wings of joy and light.
In glances sweet, our spirits rise,
As stars align to bless the night.

Echoing with whispers bold,
Every heartbeat pulses clear.
In festive tales, new joys unfold,
Creating magic we hold dear.

With every bite, flavors blend,
A feast of colors on display.
In friendship's warmth, the hours spend,
Chasing dusk into bright day.

So raise a glass to dreams in flight,
To moments cherished, bonds will grow.
In the distance of the night,
Our hearts will dance, our spirits glow.

Dreams that Stir the Stillness

In twilight's grace, the lights ignite,
Whispers of joy in the starry night.
Laughter dances, spirits bright,
Together we share this sweet delight.

Balloons afloat, in colors bold,
Stories of wonders, waiting to be told.
With every heartbeat, the warmth unfolds,
Friendship's embrace, more precious than gold.

The Pulse of Hidden Currents

Beneath the surface, the rhythms play,
Echoes of dreams in the bright display.
Joy weaves through in a lively sway,
Uniting souls in a festive array.

Glittering lights, with magic entwined,
Moments of laughter, so sweet and kind.
Together we bloom, our hearts aligned,
In this embrace, true love defined.

Tides of Change

Waves of joy crash on the shore,
New beginnings, we all adore.
Chasing laughter, we start to soar,
In this festivity, we crave for more.

Colors of dusk merge into night,
Sparkling dreams set hearts alight.
With every cheer, our spirits take flight,
Together we shine, a brilliant sight.

Ephemeral Impressions

Moments flicker like candles' glow,
Each smile a treasure, sweet and slow.
In this embrace, we feel the flow,
A tapestry woven, forever aglow.

As laughter echoes through the air,
We celebrate life without a care.
Memories painted, a canvas rare,
In this festive heart, we all share.

Fragments of an Unseen Journey

Dancing lights upon the street,
Joyful laughter fills the air,
Hands held tight in warmth so sweet,
Together, burdens we will share.

Every step a story told,
Brightly colored dreams ignite,
In our hearts, the world unfolds,
Guiding us through day and night.

Whispers of the stars above,
As we chase the fleeting glow,
Moments wrapped in endless love,
In this dance, our spirits flow.

Paths untraveled, sweet surprise,
With each heartbeat, hope will rise,
Fragments weave a tapestry,
Of unseen journeys yet to be.

Fables of Calm Waters

Beneath the arch of willow trees,
Rippling echoes gently call,
In this space, we find our ease,
As nature sings its timeless thrall.

Gentle breezes brush our skin,
Whispers dream of lore and fable,
Every moment feels akin,
To stories shared around the table.

Sunset paints the sky in hues,
Golden glimmers dance and play,
In this peace, we cannot lose,
The magic woven in the day.

With each wave, a tale unfolds,
Fables rich with joy and grace,
Calm waters, life's sweetest molds,
Reflecting smiles upon each face.

Mosaic of Soft Echoes

Shimmering lights in evening's grasp,
Each laughter a piece of art,
Moments flutter, time to clasp,
Mosaics built from every heart.

Colorful dreams in twilight's glow,
Every whisper, soft and bright,
In this blend, our souls bestow,
Echoes dancing through the night.

Stories linger, shadows play,
Casting warmth on each dear face,
In a world that spins away,
Here, we find our sacred space.

Together, we are sparks of light,
A tapestry that weaves so fine,
Mosaic of the softest night,
In every heart, a cherished sign.

Solitary Flights into Reflection

Upon the wings of twilight's breeze,
Thoughts drift high like fleeting dreams,
In solitude, the heart's at ease,
Crafting whispers, soft moonbeams.

Stars unveil their quiet glow,
Lighting paths of inward grace,
In each twinkling spark, we know,
We are not lost; just find our place.

Every shadow holds a tale,
Silent echoes, gently stirred,
In their arms, we shall not fail,
To find the truth in every word.

Solitary flights take wing,
In reflection, we ignite,
From solitude, our voices sing,
In the calm of starry night.

Movement in Stasis

Lively colors dance and swirl,
In the air, the laughter twirls.
Joyful music fills the night,
As hearts beat strong, with pure delight.

Streamers flashing in the light,
People gather, spirits bright.
With every cheer, the night ignites,
Dancing shadows fill the sights.

Footsteps echo on the ground,
Rhythms pulse, a joyful sound.
In this moment, time suspends,
A fleeting joy that never ends.

With each smile that we share,
Life's sweet magic fills the air.
In this stasis, we find grace,
Together, we embrace this space.

Shattered Calm

Stillness broken by a sound,
Laughter ripples all around.
Joyful chaos fills the void,
Echoes of the peace destroyed.

Colors burst like fireworks' flare,
Grins exchanged in blissful air.
Whispers turn to joyful cries,
As night blooms beneath the skies.

Voices lift like swirls of smoke,
In this magic, hearts evoke.
Every glance a story weaves,
As festivity believes.

Moments flicker, fleeting, bright,
In the fractures of the night.
Though calm once ruled, the spirit's free,
In shattered stillness, we find glee.

Undercurrents of Emotion

Beneath the surface, feelings flow,
Like rivers deep in twilight's glow.
Joy and laughter intertwine,
In a dance that's so divine.

Waves of cheerful banter rise,
In the air, a sweet surprise.
Faces gleam with pure delight,
Euphoria paints the night.

Tides may shift with every smile,
But in this joy, we linger awhile.
Moments shared create a spark,
Igniting life in the dark.

Undercurrents pulse with meaning,
Every heartbeat, joy redeeming.
In the festivity afloat,
We find the chords that hearts devote.

Alchemy of the Still

In quiet corners, laughter brews,
A gentle warmth in evening's hues.
Festive whispers wake the night,
Transforming calm into delight.

Bottles clink, the toast begins,
Cheers resound, as joy within spins.
Glimmers of gold from every grin,
The alchemy of life's sweet din.

In stillness, energy ignites,
Like fireworks in starry nights.
With open hearts and hands held high,
We dance beneath the vast, deep sky.

Moments merge, creating bliss,
In this stillness, love's the kiss.
A festive spell that wraps our souls,
In silent joy, we're made whole.

Awakening of the Silent

In the dawn of a bright new day,
Whispers of joy come out to play.
Colors dance in the morning light,
Hearts beat fast, spirits soar in flight.

Laughter blooms like flowers in spring,
Hope takes root, and the world will sing.
Every shadow fades into cheer,
As love and warmth draw everyone near.

The melody flows, a sweet refrain,
Every soul touched, free from all pain.
Together we stand, hands held tight,
In this moment, everything feels right.

As the sun sets, the stars will gleam,
We cherish this life, a shared dream.
With each heartbeat, our joy ignites,
Awakening love through endless nights.

When Time Takes Flight

Time flutters by like leaves in fall,
Laughter wraps 'round, inviting all.
Moments shimmer like stars above,
In this dance, we share our love.

The clock strikes joy, a sacred beat,
Every heartbeat feels so sweet.
We gather 'round in circles tight,
Holding each other, hearts alight.

Memories made in bursts of glee,
This festive air is wild and free.
We lift our voices, let them soar,
When time takes flight, we yearn for more.

With every second, magic grows,
In the ebb and flow, our spirit glows.
Together we'll paint the sky so bright,
As love and laughter take their flight.

The Subtle Art of Motion

In a room where the music plays,
Bodies sway in a joyful haze.
A gentle rhythm, a dance unseen,
The subtle art of what might have been.

Hands reach out, connect with grace,
Every smile lights up the space.
Feet tap softly on the ground,
In this moment, joy is found.

A twirl, a dip, the laughter rings,
Life is rich with the joy it brings.
With every move, a story told,
In the warmth of laughter, we are bold.

As shadows play under the lights,
We cherish these sweet, festive nights.
Together we rise, together we sway,
In the subtle art, we find our way.

Fleeting Echoes of Serenity

In the twilight, a hush descends,
Soft whispers float, the magic blends.
Stars twinkle in a cloak of peace,
Fleeting echoes that never cease.

Candles flicker, their warmth invites,
Sharing stories on cozy nights.
Laughter ripples through the air,
In this moment, we're free of care.

A gentle breeze carries sweet scents,
Every heartbeat feels like it repents.
In the quiet, joy holds sway,
Fleeting echoes, a bright ballet.

We treasure these soft, fleeting dreams,
In the heart's embrace, love redeems.
With every breath, we find serenity,
In the festive glow, we live in harmony.

Tranquil Portraits of Nature

In vibrant hues the flowers bloom,
A dance of colors bright and bold,
Beneath the sky, a peaceful room,
Where nature's canvas turns to gold.

The gentle breeze whispers a tune,
While rustling leaves sway in delight,
Under the watchful eye of the moon,
The stars emerge to greet the night.

The brook babbles soft melodies near,
A symphony of life unfolds,
Each note a cherished voice we hear,
In tranquil portraits nature holds.

With every scene, a joyous sigh,
Together we weave dreams so sweet,
In tranquil spaces where spirits fly,
A celebration, life's own heartbeat.

The Undercurrents of Serenity

The river flows, a silver thread,
Beneath the surface, whispers flow,
Secrets of peace, softly spread,
In the stillness, tranquility glows.

Mountains stand in quiet pride,
Their peaks kissed by the sun's warm grace,
In solitude, strength abides,
A serene smile on nature's face.

Waves of grass dance with the breeze,
A gentle rhythm, soft and sweet,
In this haven, hearts find ease,
In undercurrents, calm retreats.

Clouds drift lazily, no haste,
In this moment, joy is found,
Serenity, a lingering taste,
Where whispers of peace abound.

Stillness in Motion

Leaves twirl gracefully in flight,
Caught in a dance with nature's hand,
An artful display, pure delight,
Where time stands still, yet feels so grand.

Fireflies wink in twilight's glow,
Each flicker a spark of joy divine,
As stars begin their nightly show,
In the stillness, magic intertwines.

The world slows down, breathes in tune,
Harmonies of night serenade,
In this moment, hearts attune,
To the secrets that life has made.

Stillness dances, life's sweet refrain,
In every heartbeat, a vibrant song,
In motion's grace, we find no pain,
In festive spirits, we all belong.

The Elegance of Entranced Minds

In crowded rooms, we find our peace,
Laughter lingers, spirits rise,
Through conversations, joys release,
The elegance where friendship lies.

With every toast, our hearts unite,
In moments shared, we feel alive,
Within the glow of soft candlelight,
A festivity where dreams thrive.

Colors swirl, and voices blend,
Creating a tapestry of cheer,
In this dance, the heart can mend,
As every soul feels love draw near.

Life's celebrations, woven tight,
Through elegance, we find our way,
In entranced minds, the world feels bright,
In festive joy, we choose to stay.

A Canvas of Gentle Hues

Brush strokes dance in the light,
Colors twirl, spirits take flight.
Laughter weaves through the air,
Joyous whispers, everywhere.

Candles flicker, shadows play,
Brightening up a gloomy day.
Each smile paints a vibrant scene,
In this world, so lush and green.

Music flows like a gentle stream,
Flowing softly, a waking dream.
Hands come together, hearts align,
In this moment, love will shine.

Under skies painted with glee,
The night blossoms, wild and free.
Together we twirl, laugh, and sing,
In our hearts, the warmth we bring.

The Lullaby of Forgotten Moments

Stars twinkle in the midnight glow,
Whispers of time begin to flow.
Memories dance in soft embrace,
In this quiet, we find our space.

Laughter echoes in the breeze,
Tickling leaves of the ancient trees.
Every glance is a story retold,
A melody that never grows old.

Time may slip through fingers tight,
But here, it slows in the moonlight.
Each heartbeat sings a timeless tune,
As night wraps us beneath the moon.

In simple joys, treasures reside,
In gentle moments, love's great tide.
Let us linger, let us stay,
In the lullaby of yesterday.

The Gap Between Two Heartbeats

In the pause between laughter bright,
A silence echoes, pure delight.
Moments sit, hanging in air,
Breaths entwined, a perfect pair.

Fingers brush with electric thrill,
In that space, a love we build.
Time stands still, a sweet refrain,
In whispers soft, no hint of pain.

Eyes meet in a universe vast,
Dreams collide, shadowed and cast.
In that heartbeat, worlds collide,
In silence deep, where love can hide.

Dance with me in this reprieve,
In the gap, there's so much to believe.
Together we'll weave, together we'll soar,
In that fleeting pulse, forevermore.

In the Shadow of Silent Giants

Among the trees, so tall and wise,
Secrets linger beneath blue skies.
Nature hums a timeless tune,
Whispered dreams under the moon.

Leaves shimmer with every breeze,
In the hush, hearts find their ease.
Together we wander, souls awake,
In this haven, we shall make.

The giants stand, their tales untold,
Guardians of memories bold.
In their shade, we find our way,
Under stars that dance and sway.

As shadows stretch and daylight fades,
Together we'll roam through peaceful glades.
In the silence, our spirits align,
In this sanctuary, your hand in mine.

Awakened by the Stillness

In the crisp air, laughter flows,
Colors dance where the sunlight glows.
Joyful whispers fill the breeze,
Nature smiles, putting hearts at ease.

Flowers bloom in vibrant hues,
Echoing merriment in morning dew.
A gathering of friends draws near,
Together, casting away all fear.

Songs of cheer rise through the trees,
Uniting souls with gentle ease.
The world awakens, pure delight,
In the stillness, everything feels right.

Sparkling eyes reflecting dreams,
Festivities wrapped in sunny beams.
Each moment cherished, laughter shared,
In this stillness, love is declared.

The Language of Unseen Paths

In twilight's glow, the world expands,
With secret paths where joy withstands.
Footsteps whisper, hearts take flight,
In fields of hope, everything feels bright.

Laughter mingles with the stars,
Carried softly from near to far.
Every gesture, every smile,
Crafts a bond, a joyful style.

Fact and fiction blend as one,
In this calendar of endless fun.
Candles flicker, shadows dance,
In each moment lies a chance.

Together, kindred spirits sing,
To the joy that the night will bring.
In unseen paths, we find our way,
Embracing life, come what may.

When Time Stands Still

Beneath the stars, the evening glows,
With soft refrains that nature knows.
Time pauses in this dreamy space,
Where every heartbeat finds its place.

The moonlight bathes the world in gold,
A festive tale waiting to be told.
Fingers entwined, laughter flows,
In the stillness, pure joy grows.

Every glance a spark of glee,
Building memories, just you and me.
In this moment, all is well,
Each smile a story we would tell.

With every heartbeat, magic swells,
As we linger in these timeless spells.
Together we dance, as shadows play,
In this haven, we wish to stay.

The Heartbeat of Hidden Quiet

In the hush of night, secrets grow,
With whispers soft, like falling snow.
Underneath the canopy of dreams,
The world awakens, bursting at the seams.

Candles flicker with warm embrace,
Carving shadows across every face.
In every pause, a celebration,
The heartbeat of sweet anticipation.

Gentle laughter and sighs collide,
In these moments, hope can't hide.
Together we weave a tapestry bright,
In hidden quiet, hearts take flight.

Vows and wishes softly soar,
Echoing love, forevermore.
In this sanctuary, dreams ignite,
The heartbeat of quiet feels just right.

The Stillness that Speaks Volumes

In the hush of night, whispers dance,
Laughter echoes, a sweet romance.
Twinkling stars like eyes aglow,
Celebrate the magic in the flow.

Candles flicker, casting spells,
Stories shared in secret wells.
A gathering of friends so dear,
Festive hearts are drawing near.

Joyful songs on gentle breeze,
Gathered warmth puts minds at ease.
In this stillness, love unfolds,
A tapestry of moments, bold.

With every smile, a tale retold,
In the quiet, vibrant and gold.
Life's a canvas, joy the brush,
In this space, we softly hush.

Tides of Calm Between Us

In the twilight glow, we sway with ease,
The world around us hums with tease.
A sea of laughter, waves of cheer,
In the calm, our spirits steer.

The moon above, a silver gleam,
Ignites the night with a radiant beam.
With every heartbeat, joy will flow,
Where friendship thrives, love will grow.

Underneath the stars, stories spill,
In every silence, we find a thrill.
A bond that stretches like the tide,
In our hearts, the warmth won't hide.

With gentle whispers, dreams take flight,
In the calm, we find our light.
Celebration of the moments shared,
This tranquil bond, forever declared.

Secrets Hidden in Tranquility

In shaded corners, secrets lie,
Silent whispers dance and sigh.
The world outside spins fast and bright,
Yet here we treasure pure delight.

Colors burst in every glance,
Festive hearts amidst the chance.
In hidden nooks, laughter rings,
A symphony of simple things.

Quiet joys in the evening glow,
Hiding treasures only we know.
With every smile, a secret keeps,
In tranquility, our spirit leaps.

Beneath the stars, we softly share,
The magic woven in the air.
In stillness, what we find and seek,
Are precious gems, the joyous peak.

The Light Beyond the Veil of Quiet

Where silence reigns, there's vibrant light,
A festive spark that feels so right.
It dances softly on the breeze,
Bringing warmth and joyful ease.

In the depth of night, stars ignite,
Painting dreams in shades of light.
With every twinkle, love appears,
A gathering of hopes and cheers.

Here in the calm, our hearts align,
In whispers, every voice does shine.
Together wrapped in peace so sweet,
In this embrace, our souls complete.

The veil of quiet, a canvas bare,
Colored with laughter, love, and care.
In joyful moments, we break through,
The light beyond shines bright and true.

The Whispering Meadow

In the meadow where laughter plays,
Sunshine dances through the rays.
Colors bloom in joyful cheer,
Nature's symphony, sweet and clear.

Friends gather under skies so wide,
With every heart, excitement inside.
Flowers swaying in gentle breeze,
Bringing warmth and endless ease.

Sweet scents linger in the air,
Gleeful moments everywhere.
Chasing dreams on vibrant ground,
In this place, joy is profound.

As twilight wraps the day in gold,
Stories cherished, forever told.
In the whispering meadow's delight,
Hearts unite, oh, what a sight!

Footprints in the Stillness

On the shore where oceans meet,
Footprints dance, a rhythm sweet.
Waves caress with gentle grace,
Time stands still in this embrace.

Beneath a sky painted in hue,
Sunsets whisper secrets new.
Laughter echoes, hearts entwined,
Unwritten tales, a love defined.

Stars begin their twinkling song,
In this stillness, we belong.
Fires crackle, warmth surrounds,
In every moment, joy abounds.

As shadows stretch and night takes flight,
Each shared glance, a fleeting light.
Footprints fade, but love remains,
In the stillness, joy sustains.

The Gentle Push of Time

Seasons change with a subtle sigh,
Moments drift as clouds float by.
Time's gentle hand guides our way,
Through laughter shared, come what may.

Every tick, a heartbeat felt,
In the warmth of love, we melt.
Sunrise paints the world anew,
With every dawn, dreams come true.

Memories blossoming like spring,
In the joy that sunshine brings.
With every moment, life in bloom,
Echoes of festivity loom.

Together we savor the flight,
In this dance, we find our light.
The gentle push of time we share,
Whispers of joy fill the air.

Traces of the Unheard Call

In the forest where secrets lie,
Traces linger, whispers sigh.
Nature's voice, soft and inviting,
In the shadows, dreams igniting.

Moonlight bathes the leaves in glow,
Magic stirs in currents slow.
Stars above twinkle with glee,
Promising wonders yet to see.

Footsteps echo on the trail,
Adventure waiting, never pale.
With friends beside us, journeys start,
In every heartbeat, joy imparts.

As dawn approaches, dreams take flight,
With every laugh, the world feels right.
Traces left by unseen hands,
In their magic, joy expands.

The Unraveled Thread of Serenity

In the glow of lantern light,
Laughter dances through the air,
Colors blend in joyous flight,
Stitching memories to share.

Breezes hum a gentle tune,
Hearts entwined in festive cheer,
Moonbeams waltz with silver soon,
Whispers soft to draw us near.

Each moment like a treasure,
Unraveled threads of gold so bright,
Weaving warmth in heartfelt pleasure,
Embracing magic, fleeting night.

Hands upraised, the stars comply,
On this thread, we weave our dreams,
Sailing forth, we kiss the sky,
In the wake of joy, we gleam.

Surrendering to the Soft Embrace

Underneath the swaying trees,
Laughter spills like honeyed wine,
In the warm, inviting breeze,
Hearts gather and intertwine.

Candles flicker, shadows play,
Echoes of a distant song,
Night succumbs to bright ballet,
As we dance, we all belong.

With every smile, a spark ignites,
Filling air with sweet delight,
Embracing dreams and starlit nights,
In this moment, all feels right.

Soft embraces, gentle sighs,
Plucking strings of joy and grace,
Together under vast, clear skies,
Surrender, lose all sense of place.

Celestial Whispers at Dusk

When twilight cloaks the day in pink,
The stars begin their playful dance,
Each blink a flicker, beckoning link,
To the moonlit night's vast expanse.

In gatherings, friends unite,
Candles lit like constellations,
With every laugh, the world feels bright,
Creating shared elation.

Silhouettes under a violet hue,
Hands raised high in sheer delight,
Whispers carry, old and new,
Painting dreams that take to flight.

As the night begins to hum,
Hope ignites in hearts so true,
In this magic, we become,
A cosmic tapestry in view.

Elysium of the Unnoticed

In gardens where soft petals fall,
Laughter weaves a silken thread,
With every echo, joy stands tall,
Creating paths where love is spread.

The sun dips low, a painted sky,
Colors merge and kiss the ground,
As daylight waves its sweet goodbye,
In the dusk, our dreams are found.

Secrets whispered in the breeze,
Moments clad in gentle grace,
In the night, we own our keys,
Unlocking doors to time and space.

In this Elysium unseen,
We gather in the stillness here,
Each heartbeat echoes what has been,
In the unnoticed, we find cheer.

The Gentle Unraveling

Balloons float high, colors in the sky,
Laughter ringing clear, sweet as a sigh.
Candles flicker softly, their glow like a friend,
Whispers of joy as the evening descends.

Tables adorned with treasures so bright,
Each heart is a lantern, glowing with light.
Songs of the season dance on the air,
Moments together, nothing can compare.

Frosted treats sparkle like starlit dreams,
While children chase fireflies, or so it seems.
Every hug cherished, every toast raised high,
Under the blanket of a velvety sky.

Time slips away, like grains in the sand,
In this gentle unraveling, we take a stand.
Together we weave a tapestry grand,
In the warmth of our gathering, hand in hand.

Whispers of the Unseen

A breeze carries secrets that flutter and play,
Among the tall trees where the shadows sway.
Invisible wonders embrace the night air,
Whispers of magic linger everywhere.

Moonlight spills silver on leaves soft and green,
Painting a picture of sights yet unseen.
Fireflies twinkle, a delicate dance,
Nature's own rhythm, inviting romance.

The sound of contentment, soft laughter rings,
As friends share their stories, the joy that it brings.
Together we gather beneath twinkling skies,
In this festive haven, our spirits arise.

With each gentle murmur, the world comes alive,
In the heart of the moment, we truly thrive.
Hand in hand, we'll treasure the night,
In whispers of unseen, we find our delight.

Echoes of Tranquil Winds

The gentle wind carries a soothing refrain,
A melody woven through fields of grain.
Sunsets blush softly with hues warm and bold,
As day melts to twilight, a magic unfold.

Gathered together, our hearts beat in sync,
Shared stories flow like a luminous drink.
Under the stars, we let worries take flight,
Embracing the calm on this festive night.

The sounds of the forest, a symphony sweet,
Rustling leaves dance with the rhythm of feet.
In laughter and joy, we paint the night sky,
In the echoes of winds, our spirits can fly.

With every soft whisper that brushes our face,
We weave into friendship a warm, cozy space.
Just like the breeze that caresses the ground,
In tranquil moments, our happiness found.

The Dance of Silent Waters

Beneath the moon's gaze, the waters do sway,
Ripples of laughter reflect the soft play.
In the stillness of night, the world fades away,
As we gather our dreams beneath stars' array.

The dance of the waters whispers sweet songs,
Timeless and tender, where each heart belongs.
Floating on wishes, our spirits unite,
In the festivity wrapped in a shimmering light.

Candlelit glimmers adorn paths we tread,
Stories unfold as the echoes are spread.
With every soft splash, we share in delight,
As the dance of the waters brings peace to the night.

Together we sparkle like stars from above,
A tapestry woven with laughter and love.
In this festive embrace, where memories soar,
The dance of silent waters forever will pour.

The Pulse of Hidden Currents

Beneath the surface, laughter swells,
Whispers dance where magic dwells.
Colors twirl in vibrant streams,
The pulse of life ignites our dreams.

Stars above in shimmering array,
Guide our hearts to join the play.
Every smile a fleeting spark,
Lighting up the evening dark.

In hidden corners, secrets sigh,
As echoes of joy flutter by.
The world a canvas, splashed with cheer,
In this moment, magic is near.

Together we weave, a tapestry bright,
In the pulse of currents, we take flight.
With every heartbeat, we are alive,
In the festive spirit, our souls thrive.

Fleeting Moments of Solitude

In quiet corners where shadows play,
Soft whispers linger, keeping doubts at bay.
A brief escape in a world of haste,
Finding peace in the moment's taste.

The candle flickers, a gentle glow,
Illuminating thoughts that flow.
Lost in reverie, time stands still,
In fleeting silence, we find our will.

Outside, the laughter calls and sings,
The pulse of life in vibrant wings.
Yet here we dwell, in calm retreat,
With memories cherished, our hearts beat.

So let us savor these fleeting times,
As joy weaves through with silent rhymes.
In solitude, festive sparks ignite,
A celebration of the inner light.

In the Wake of Forgotten Echoes

Old melodies drift on the breeze,
Recalling tales that time could seize.
In the wake of echoes, laughter wakes,
Bringing joy for memory's sake.

With every note, a past reborn,
In festive colors, we are adorned.
Stories shared in the glow of night,
We forge connections, hold them tight.

Amidst the shadows, warmth draws near,
In whispered songs that only we hear.
Each heartbeat swells with timeless grace,
In the dance of moments, we find our place.

So let these echoes softly chime,
A celebration of love, through all of time.
In the wake of joy, we rise and blend,
Together we find, our hearts transcend.

Still Waters Run Deep

Upon the surface, the world may gleam,
Yet still waters hold a secret dream.
In quiet depths, reflections grow,
A tranquil pulse, a vibrant flow.

Beneath the calm, a heartbeat lies,
Winding whispers, connecting ties.
In gentle ripples, joy unfurls,
As festive laughter dances and swirls.

The night embraces, cool and bright,
Mirroring stars with pure delight.
In silent waters, the spirit thrives,
In every stillness, the heart revives.

So come and share this tranquil space,
Where still waters reveal their grace.
In every moment, let us leap,
For in our depths, the pulse runs deep.

Repose in the Shadows of Nature

Beneath the trees, we laugh and play,
Whispers of breezes dance our way.
In dappled light, we find our cheer,
Nature's embrace, so warm and near.

With petals soft, the flowers bloom,
Colors burst, dispelling gloom.
A picnic spread on grassy floor,
Joyful hearts forever soar.

Birds serenade the azure sky,
Their melodies make spirits fly.
In every rustle, secrets sigh,
We gather warmth as shadows lie.

Golden rays as daylight fades,
Our laughter weaves through twilight glades.
Here in the shadows, love does trace,
A festive spirit we embrace.

Celestial Bodies in Quiet Convergence

Stars ignite the velvet night,
Whispers of dreams, a wondrous sight.
Planets dance in cosmic flow,
A symphony of light we know.

The moonlight glows, a silver hue,
Reflecting hope in all we do.
Galaxies twirl in joyous play,
A festive night to drift away.

Constellations paint the skies,
Winking brightly, soft lullabies.
With every twinkle, wishes bloom,
As night enfolds with sweet perfume.

In quiet moments, hearts connect,
Celestial love we all reflect.
In unity, our spirits soar,
Together, we find so much more.

Embracing the Space Between

In every glance, a spark ignites,
A bond that shines through starry nights.
With every laugh, we weave a thread,
In silken whispers, softly said.

The joy of presence fills the air,
In moments shared, we dare to care.
Each heartbeat echoes, rich and bright,
A tapestry of pure delight.

With hands entwined, we move as one,
Under the warmth of golden sun.
The space between, a dance we make,
With every step, the world we wake.

In shared silence, love's embrace,
Together we find our sacred space.
Festive hearts, forever free,
In this magic, you and me.

The Sound of Delicate Moments

The rustle of leaves in gentle breeze,
A melody that aims to please.
Laughter echoes through the trees,
In every note, the soul's release.

Soft whispers float on evening air,
Promises echoed everywhere.
As twilight wraps the earth in lace,
We linger here, in joyful space.

The tinkling chimes from distant hills,
A symphony that gently thrills.
In fragile moments, hearts embrace,
Together weaving light's sweet grace.

As night descends, the stars align,
While magic sparkles, pure and fine.
In every sound, we come alive,
In delicate moments, we thrive.

The Stillness that Breathes

In the glow of the lantern's light,
Joy dances with shadows' delight,
Laughter spills like sparkling wine,
Moments cherished, hearts align.

Beneath the stars, whispers unfold,
Stories of warmth, both new and old,
Hands interlocked, a soft embrace,
Together we revel in this space.

Colors swirl in the evening sky,
Dreams ignite, like fireworks high,
The night hums with a jubilant tune,
While fairy lights twinkle at the moon.

In every heartbeat, a rhythm sings,
Celebration blooms in the joy it brings,
Softly now, the world slows down,
Wrapped in the magic, we wear the crown.

Unraveling the Threads of Silence

In the hush where laughter brews,
We weave the night with vibrant hues,
Every whisper, a gentle thread,
Tales of friendship, joy widespread.

Candles flicker, casting soft light,
Embracing warmth of the festive night,
Dancing shadows blend and sway,
In this moment, we drift away.

As stars awaken above the trees,
Our spirits lifted, carried by breeze,
The world spins in a sweet refrain,
Joy shines bright, we ease the strain.

Unraveling secrets beneath the glow,
Diary pages of laughter flow,
In silence shared, the heartbeats rise,
Fragmented dreams become the prize.

Shadows of a Quiet Dawn

Morning breaks with a gentle sigh,
Awakening dreams that fill the sky,
Colors spread, a painter's brush,
In nature's stillness, hearts do hush.

Soft rays stroke the waking earth,
Every moment, a joyful birth,
Whispers of hope dance in the air,
A celebration, serene and rare.

The world bathes in golden light,
Promises shimmer in the bright,
Holding hands, we greet the day,
In harmony, we find our way.

With every step, we spark delight,
In the shadows of this quiet light,
Together we dream, together we sing,
In this dawn, a sense of spring.

Reflections in a Still Lake

By the shore where waters gleam,
Mirrors hold a tranquil dream,
Ripples dance in the gentle breeze,
Echoing life in soft decrees.

Every glance reveals the heart,
In stillness' calm, we play our part,
Moments captured, memories made,
In the lake's embrace, we wade.

Laughter bounces off the waves,
In the calm, our spirit braves,
A kaleidoscope of joy unfolds,
Reflections brighter than golds.

We gather close beneath the sun,
In every ripple, we're all one,
With hearts alight, our souls set free,
In the still lake, we find harmony.

The Veil of Quietude

In whispers soft, the night does twirl,
A tapestry of stars unfurl.
Laughter dances, warm and bright,
As shadows blend with twinkling light.

Beneath the moon's enchanting glow,
We share our dreams, let feelings flow.
With gentle hearts, the world slows down,
In tranquil moments, joy is found.

Candles flicker in the breeze,
Mellow music, a sweet tease.
Together we weave stories shared,
In this embrace, none are spared.

So let us bask, as spirits lift,
In quietude, love is our gift.
With every giggle, every sigh,
Under the veil of night, we fly.

Embracing the Unrushed

In morning light, the world awakes,
With smiles as the daylight breaks.
Breezes linger, time slows down,
In vibrant fields, we lose our frown.

Cups raised high, the laughter flows,
As gratitude in each heart grows.
We stroll through moments rich and free,
In simple joys, we find our glee.

Colors burst in every sight,
As spirits dance in pure delight.
With friends around, no need to hurry,
In this embrace, there's no worry.

So let us breathe the day so slow,
In every heartbeat, love will grow.
Embracing time as sweet and grand,
Together here, we take our stand.

Revelations in Silence

In silence deep, the stars unfold,
An ancient tale that needs retold.
With unspoken words, we connect,
In every glance, we find respect.

The stillness sings a soothing song,
Where dreams and hopes can both belong.
With every pause, the beauty flows,
In whispered thoughts, true magic grows.

Eyes that twinkle, hearts that share,
A festival of souls laid bare.
In quietude, the world's aglow,
In the silence, love will show.

So let us cherish this sweet grace,
In moments still, we find our place.
A canvas painted in pure light,
Revelations bloom in the night.

Secrets of the Unseen

Beyond the veil, the secrets lie,
In shared delight, we laugh and sigh.
With playful glances, bonds we tie,
As joy and wonder fill the sky.

In corners hidden, whispers dwell,
Of joy and peace, we weave our spell.
With every step, our spirits soar,
In unity, we crave for more.

The night unfolds with tales untold,
In every heartbeat, warmth we hold.
With light around, we dare to dream,
As laughter bursts like a bright beam.

So join the dance of life and cheer,
In every moment, love draws near.
With secrets shared and hearts so free,
In festivity, we find the key.

Whispers of Movement

In the glow of twinkling lights,
Laughter echoes through the nights.
Feet twirl on the cobblestone,
Joy is felt in every tone.

Colors blend in vibrant hues,
Festive spirits, hearts renew.
Voices rise, a joyful cheer,
Every moment sings so dear.

The air is filled with sweet delight,
As friends gather, hearts ignite.
Wonders dance in every breeze,
Embracing life with perfect ease.

Through the night, we share our dreams,
Under stars, the starlight beams.
Together, let our spirits fly,
In this moment, you and I.

Echoes in the Silence

Underneath the budding trees,
Whispers float upon the breeze.
Silent nights wrapped in delight,
Stars above, a twinkling sight.

Candles flicker, shadows play,
Moments cherished, come what may.
Stories told in hushed tones,
Hearts transformed, a place called home.

Laughter lingers, softly fades,
In the dark, our joy cascades.
Hope ignites like morning light,
Bringing warmth to quiet night.

In the stillness, we all sway,
Finding peace in our ballet.
Echoes linger, sweet and clear,
A festive call that draws us near.

The Dance of Forgotten Moments

In the twilight, memories sway,
Dancing shadows, come what may.
Softly woven through the years,
The laughter echoes, dries the tears.

Familiar tunes float on the air,
Every heartbeat, we can share.
Brightened faces, glowing eyes,
A tapestry of joyous ties.

As the night embraces all,
Let us rise and heed the call.
In the rhythm of the night,
We find solace, pure delight.

With every step, we're not alone,
In this dance, our spirits grown.
Together lost in festive play,
In the moment, come what may.

Ripples in the Calm

Beneath the moon, the waters gleam,
Reflections bright, a silver dream.
Gentle waves in soft embrace,
A tranquil world, a festive space.

Intertwined, we share our tales,
As laughter over water sails.
Moments captured, hearts entwined,
In the stillness, joy we find.

The night unfolds like a warm hug,
Every heart beats, every shrug.
In the calm, the ripples play,
As dreams twirl in a grand ballet.

With every cheer, the spirits rise,
Underneath the starry skies.
In peaceful joy, we celebrate,
The ripples dance, we resonate.

A Journey Through Calm Seas

Waves lap gently, a soft embrace,
Sunlight dances, lighting each space.
Seagulls call in joyous flight,
Every moment feels just right.

Sailing forth on a tranquil tide,
Hope and laughter, we take in stride.
The ocean's whispers fill the air,
A journey cherished, a bond we share.

Colors blend in hues so bright,
With every sunset, comes pure delight.
Stars twinkle overhead, a guide,
Together we sail, hearts open wide.

Adventure awaits beyond the shore,
With each wave, we yearn for more.
A celebration of life and dreams,
On calm seas, the world gleams.

Nestled in the Arms of Time

Golden moments draped in sighs,
The clock ticks softly, love never dies.
Memories swirl in a tender embrace,
In the stillness, we've found our place.

Laughter echoes, warm and clear,
Seasons change, but we hold dear.
In every heartbeat, joy unfolds,
Nestled in stories yet untold.

Time's gentle hand weaves each thread,
A tapestry formed by the paths we've tread.
Present glimmers with the past's sweet chimes,
Together we dance, nestled in time.

With every glance, our spirits soar,
In this sanctuary, we seek to explore.
A festive celebration of who we are,
Shining bright like the evening star.

Layers of Soft Light

Morning breaks with a gentle glow,
Petals open, their colors flow.
The world awakens, fresh and bright,
Wrapped in layers of soft light.

Laughter spills like sunbeams free,
Shadows play beneath the tree.
Children dance, their spirits so free,
In every heart, sweet jubilee.

Twilight drapes its velvet cloth,
With every star, connections froth.
Layer upon layer, a festive sight,
As dreams unfold in the soft light.

An evening's cheer, a joyful share,
Together we breathe the vibrant air.
In layers bright, in colors bold,
Our stories weave, our hearts unfold.

The Serenity Beneath the Noise

In the chaos, stillness finds a way,
Whispers of peace in the midst of play.
Beneath the laughter, a calming stream,
A sanctuary born from a shared dream.

City lights flicker, the heartbeat loud,
Yet in the midst, we stand so proud.
Connections bloom where the wild winds blow,
Finding solace in the vibrant flow.

Voices mingle, a melody sweet,
Every note makes the day feel complete.
In joyful gatherings, we fuse and blend,
The serenity found in the noise we send.

With every hug, the world feels near,
Each shared moment, a reason to cheer.
In the hustle and bustle, love's gentle choice,
We discover the calm in the storm's wild voice.

Ribbons of Twilight Mist

Twilight dances in the air,
Ribbons of colour, free and fair.
Laughter echoes, joy descends,
As night's embrace softly blends.

Stars awaken, twinkling bright,
Guiding us through gentle night.
Garlands of dreams breeze along,
Together we sing, heart and song.

Candles flicker, casting cheer,
Whispers of love linger near.
In this moment, we unite,
Wrapped in warmth, no end in sight.

With every cheer, we lift our glass,
To memories sweet that ever last.
Ribbons of twilight, hand in hand,
In this festive wonderland.

Gazing Into the Quiet Abyss

Gazing into the quiet blue,
Whispers of waves, a soothing hue.
Twinkling lights, a distant shore,
In this magic, we long for more.

Laughter dances on the breeze,
Tickling senses, hearts at ease.
The moon hangs low, a guiding light,
In the stillness, all feels right.

Echoes of joy swirl in the air,
Moments of bliss beyond compare.
Gathered together, eyes aglow,
In the abyss, love starts to grow.

With stars above like diamonds clear,
We toast to dreams that bring us near.
A celebration of all that's true,
Gazing together, just me and you.

The Invisible Threads We Weave

Invisible threads connect our hearts,
Ties of devotion, in quiet parts.
Together we gather, for laughter and song,
Binding our spirits, where we belong.

Colors of joy in every embrace,
Woven in moments, a sacred space.
With every smile, a stitch we make,
Memories crafted for kindness' sake.

Around the table, stories unfold,
Tales of adventure, recollections bold.
Threads of our past with futures entwine,
In the tapestry of love, we shine.

With cups raised high, we honor the night,
In the warmth of friendship, everything's bright.
The invisible threads that tie us tight,
Sparkle like stars in endless light.

Nature's Embrace of Stillness

In nature's arms, stillness lies,
Where peace emerges, soft as sighs.
Leaves rustle gently, a whispering tune,
Under the watch of a silvery moon.

Golden sunbeams paint the ground,
In every corner, magic is found.
Birds serenade with songs so sweet,
In this haven, life feels complete.

Joy unfolds in every hue,
Dancing lights in the morning dew.
Together we roam, hand in hand,
In nature's embrace, we make our stand.

With laughter shared beneath the trees,
We lift our spirits in the summer breeze.
In the stillness, we find delight,
Nature's embrace, heartwarming and bright.

Dreams Adrift in Quietude

In a garden where laughter flows,
Balloons dance under the sun's glow.
Whispers of joy paint the skies,
As warm breezes carry sweet sighs.

Glowing lights twinkle in the night,
With music that sparkles, pure delight.
Joyful hearts gather, smiles abound,
In this paradise, love is found.

Feasts laid out, colors so bright,
With stories shared by candlelight.
Each moment a treasure, a soft embrace,
In dreams adrift, we find our place.

Laughter and dancing merge as one,
Celebrating life, a race well run.
In this haven, where spirits soar,
We hold each other and ask for more.

Horizons of Unspoken Thoughts

Beneath a sky of twinkling stars,
We share our dreams, erasing scars.
The night whispers secrets, so profound,
As hearts resonate, a vibrant sound.

With every cheer, the world feels light,
As voices blend in pure delight.
Shadows of doubt fade into the past,
In the warmth of friendship, we are steadfast.

Colors swirl in a dance divine,
As laughter weaves through every line.
Time may flutter, but we stand tall,
In horizons vast, we heed the call.

Together, we craft a tapestry bright,
In unspoken thoughts, we find our light.
A celebration of hopes that intertwine,
In this festive moment, our souls align.

Drifting Through the Loom of Time

Moments weave like threads of gold,
As stories of joy and laughter unfold.
Each tick of the clock, a memory spun,
In the fabric of life, we become one.

Dance of shadows beneath the moon,
Echoes of friendship, a lively tune.
With each heartbeat, we cherish the beat,
In this grand parade, we find our feet.

Colors blend in a festive glow,
As rivers of happiness gently flow.
Time may drift, but we hold it dear,
In gatherings bright, there's no place for fear.

So let the night carry our dreams,
In the light of love, everything gleams.
With hearts entwined, we'll weave our fate,
Embracing the joy that we create.

Murmurs Beneath the Surface

Whispers of laughter rise on the breeze,
As hearts connect with gentle ease.
In the stillness, joy softly stirs,
With murmurings sweet, the world purrs.

Glimmers of hope in every glance,
As spirits sway in a merry dance.
The air hums with promise, so clear,
In the festival's pulse, we draw near.

With every smile, we light the way,
Turning ordinary moments to play.
Beneath the surface, our dreams take flight,
In shimmering echoes, we find our light.

So let the night blanket us warm,
In the rhythm of life, we find our charm.
Murmurs of peace wrap us tight,
In this festive joy, everything feels right.

A Tapestry of Calm Whispers

In laughter's embrace, colors blend,
Joy dances lightly, a sweet, warm trend.
Balloons drift softly, a gentle flight,
Every face beaming, hearts shining bright.

Melodies float on a soft, warm breeze,
Voices intertwine among the tall trees.
Table set grand with delights to share,
Love wraps around us, a gift so rare.

Beneath the stars, the lanterns glow,
A night of wonder, where dreams overflow.
Friends gather round, their spirits alive,
In this tapestry, we all truly thrive.

With each passing hour, the laughter expands,
Moments magic, like grains of soft sands.
Together we linger, as time starts to slow,
A festive reminder of all we bestow.

The Radiance of Silence

In the hush of twilight, a shimmer appears,
Soft whispers of night, dissolve all our fears.
The world slows down, a beautiful sight,
In silence, we find our own gentle light.

Candles flicker, casting warmth on our face,
The air is aglow, wrapped in a warm embrace.
Laughter bubbles up, like champagne's sweet cheer,
In this quiet moment, we hold each other near.

Underneath the cosmos, wishes are made,
Stars twinkle brightly, a serenade played.
Time's slow rhythm sways with sweet grace,
In the radiance of silence, we find our space.

Dreams swirl around like leaves in the fall,
Each tiny sparkle ignites and enthralls.
Together we linger, hearts breaking the mold,
In this enchanted silence, our stories unfold.

Beneath the Surface of Wanting

In the vibrant crowd, a pulse fills the air,
Hearts beat like drums, syncing moments we share.
Hands raised in mirth, as the music ignites,
Joy spills like colors in festival lights.

Beneath all the laughter, a whisper resides,
A yearning for more, where desire abides.
We dance through the night, shadows softly sway,
Embracing each moment, come what may.

Glittering dreams float on laughter's refrain,
Each heartbeat echoes, a sweet, wild gain.
In fleeting desire, we're both lost and found,
Together we wander, on this joyful ground.

Fingers entwined, as the stars start to gleam,
In the depths of wanting, we chase every dream.
A festival of hopes, on this magical night,
Together we shine, in the soft, glowing light.

Chasing the Calm Before the Storm

In the vibrant dusk, the colors ignite,
Anticipation stirs, with a promise of night.
Laughter cascades, like waves on the shore,
A fleeting moment, we dare to explore.

The skies whisper secrets, a gentle embrace,
As we dance in the shadows, finding our place.
The music surrounds us, a tide, sweet and warm,
Holding the magic, before the wild storm.

Hands painted with dreams, a canvas alive,
In this tranquil pause, our spirits will thrive.
The world holds its breath, anticipating the play,
In the calm of this moment, we cherish today.

With each laughter echo, our hearts start to soar,
We're chasing the calm, before life's great roar.
Together, we linger on this turning point,
In the warmth of the now, let our souls anoint.

When Shadows Speak Softly

In a corner where laughter blooms,
Whispers dance beneath the moon.
Colors twirl in vibrant dreams,
As shadows hum their tender tunes.

Balloons drift in the evening breeze,
Children's laughter fills the trees.
Fireflies wink, a spark of light,
In this joyous, magical night.

Voices rise like sweet refrain,
Hearts unite, no hint of pain.
Celebrate this glowing thread,
Where every tear has gently fled.

So raise a glass to all we've found,
In every heartbeat, love is crowned.
When shadows speak softly, we see,
The festivity that sets us free.

Glimmers of Calm in a Chaotic World

In the hustle, find your peace,
Glimmers spark, and troubles cease.
A gentle breeze, a playful sigh,
Moments dance and softly fly.

Urban lights grind and clash,
Yet hope gleams in every flash.
Take a breath, let spirits soar,
Infinite joy opens a door.

Each heartbeat plays a radiant tune,
Under the gaze of a silvery moon.
Weaving tales with every glance,
In the chaos, let us dance.

Celebrate the small delights,
In the day and in the nights.
Glimmers of calm, hold them near,
In this world, let's spread our cheer.

Awakening the Quietude

In the dawn where dreams still weave,
Whispers softly plead, believe.
Nature yawns with gentle grace,
Awakening, we find our place.

Morning light, a tender hue,
Paints the world in colors new.
Birds greet the day with songs so bright,
Filling hearts with pure delight.

Each moment savored, draws us near,
In quietude, we find no fear.
Breathe in peace, let worries fade,
In this stillness, hope is made.

Celebrate the calm we seek,
With every breath, let love speak.
Awakening the tranquil shade,
In gentle waves, our dreams are laid.

Still Waters and Starlit Skies

Reflecting dreams on waters clear,
Stars like diamonds, drawing near.
A calming hush drapes the night,
Guiding souls in gentle flight.

Stillness sings in the world around,
Peaceful moments, magic found.
Underneath the velvet dome,
Heartbeats echo, calling home.

Every glance stars do embrace,
Holding secrets in their space.
Silent wishes sail above,
Cradling all that we hold love.

So let us gather, hand in hand,
Beneath the sky, we'll make our stand.
For still waters and starlit skies,
Carry whispers where hope lies.

Solace in the Embrace of Night

Stars twinkle brightly in the sky,
Soft whispers dance as fireflies fly.
The moon casts shadows, gentle embrace,
In this quiet moment, we find our space.

Laughter floats on the evening breeze,
Joyful hearts sway like the swaying trees.
Under the canopy of twinkling lights,
We cherish the calm that wraps us tight.

With each heartbeat, the night feels alive,
In this warm gathering, spirits thrive.
Together we share stories and dreams,
In solace we find our radiant gleams.

Embraced by night, we revel in cheer,
The world feels still, yet the joy is near.
In the magic tide of the night's gentle call,
We celebrate together, united, enthralled.

Gentle Ripples of Thought

A river of dreams flows softly by,
Casting reflections that catch the eye.
Thoughts like pebbles skip on the stream,
Gently they echo, weaving our dream.

Bright blooms awaken in the morning light,
Colors burst forth, a stunning sight.
In playful whispers, nature sings,
Under the sun, our laughter springs.

Time flows like water, serene and pure,
In its embrace, our hopes endure.
Together we gather, intentions bright,
Creating ripples in our shared delight.

With every heartbeat, we intertwine,
In a dance of joy, like sun and wine.
Embracing the moments as they unfold,
We weave our tapestry, bright and bold.

The Quiet Symphony of Nature

A gentle breeze stirs the quiet trees,
Nature composes its symphonies.
Birds chirp sweetly, a melodious cheer,
Awakening hearts as the melodies steer.

Sunlight dapples the forest floor,
Nature's treasures open each door.
Every rustle, every hush, each sigh,
Plays a note in the concert of the sky.

Together we sit, in stillness profound,
Listening closely to the softest sound.
The rhythm of leaves, the pulse of the earth,
Fills us with wonder, serenity's birth.

In this peaceful haven, we find our tune,
Under the watchful eye of the moon.
A quiet symphony weaves through the air,
Inviting our spirits to dance and share.

Where Silence Meets the Sky

At dusk, the colors blend and flow,
A canvas of dreams in warm afterglow.
Clouds drift lazily, soft as a sigh,
Where silence lingers, meeting the sky.

Stars begin to pierce the twilight's cloak,
Whispers of wishes, softly they poke.
In this hush, we breathe, hearts align,
Under the tapestry, our souls intertwine.

The horizon blushes in hues of gold,
A sight so precious, a story untold.
In this serene realm, we linger awhile,
Finding our joy in the evening's smile.

As night fully falls, we revel in peace,
In the quiet embrace, our hearts find release.
Where silence speaks volumes, soft whispers sigh,
We find our solace where silence meets sky.

www.ingramcontent.com/pod-product-compliance
Ingram Content Group UK Ltd.
Pitfield, Milton Keynes, MK11 3LW, UK
UKHW020123171224
452675UK00014BA/1535